The Roman World

Today we live in a world where everywhere is linked by telephones, TV and the Internet. Planes, trucks and cars move things about quickly. It's all one world.

The Ancient Romans made one world more than two thousand years ago. They built cities and roads, and made laws and money for everyone.

The Roman ways are still alive. We copy Roman buildings, Roman writing and Roman months. How did all this begin?

The Arc de Triomphe in Paris looks just like a Roman arch. Can you find any more arches in this book?

How Rome Grew

The first Romans lived about 2,750 years ago. Most were farmers, and they lived by the seven hills that are in the centre of Rome today.

Kings ruled Rome at first, but the rich Romans did not like this. They got rid of the last king and ruled in his place. A group of them, called the Senate, made the new laws. Each year, it chose two leaders for Rome.

In a Roman story, the first king of Rome was Romulus. Romulus and his brother Remus were brought up by a she-wolf.

READING ABOUT

Ancient
Romans

David Jay

Aladdin/Watts
London • Sydney

Contents

This edition published in 2003

© Aladdin Books Ltd 2000

Designed and produced by
Aladdin Books Ltd
28 Percy Street
London W1T 2BZ

*First published in
Great Britain in 2000 by*
Franklin Watts
96 Leonard Street
London EC2A 4XD

ISBN 0 7496 5081 8

All rights reserved

Printed in U.A.E.

Editor: Jim Pipe

Historical Consultant
Dr Rhiannon Ash

Series Literacy Consultant
Wendy Cobb

Design
Flick, Book Design and Graphics

Picture Research
Brooks Krikler Research

*A catalogue record for this book is
available from the British Library.*

For 450 years, Rome was a country without a king. This is called a republic.

These leaders had to rule well. If they didn't, no one voted for them the next year.

Rome built up an empire over hundreds of years. In an empire, one strong country rules many other countries.

Hannibal even took elephants across the Alps.

Step by step, the Romans won lands in Italy, Spain and France. They also fought long wars against the people of Carthage in North Africa.

The leader of Carthage was Hannibal. He crossed the Alp Mountains with an army. He even reached Rome. In the end, the Romans beat him and burned down Carthage.

The Romans took money and goods from all the places they captured. Money poured into Rome, making it very rich.

The Roman army leaders also grew in power. The most powerful of all was Julius Caesar. But many people thought that Caesar was greedy and wanted to make himself king.

Some members of the Senate decided to murder Caesar. They surrounded him in the Senate building and stabbed him to death.

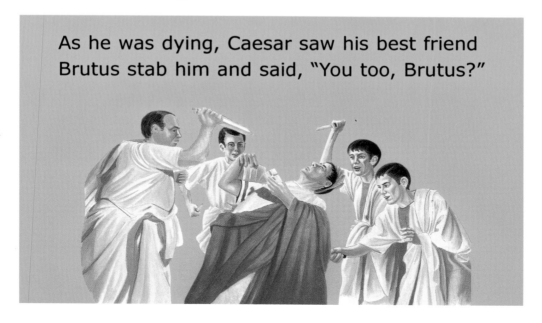

As he was dying, Caesar saw his best friend Brutus stab him and said, "You too, Brutus?"

After Caesar's death, the Romans fought among themselves for 13 years. At last, Augustus, the great-nephew of Julius Caesar, became the leader of Rome.

From now on, Rome was ruled by only one man — the emperor. Some emperors, like Hadrian and Trajan, ruled well. They brought peace to the empire or won new lands.

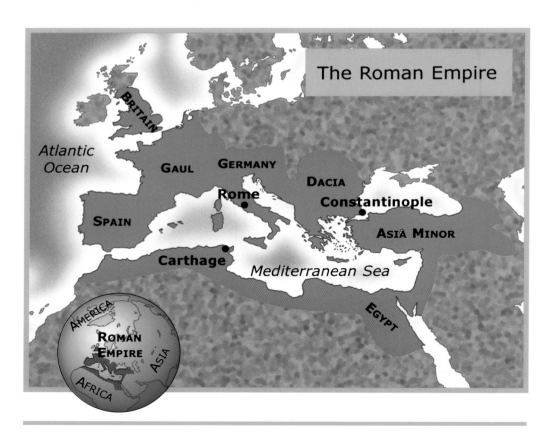

Long walls protected the empire.

Not all emperors were good rulers. The Emperor Caligula (say "ka-lig-you-la") was a bit mad. He thought he was a god, and made his horse a member of the Senate!

Under most emperors the Roman empire was a peaceful place to live. A ring of thick walls and deep ditches kept enemies out.

People inside the empire had to obey the Roman laws and the emperor. If they didn't like it, they couldn't do anything. The Roman army was too strong.

The army was split into groups of about 5,000 men, called legions. As well as fighting, the legions built roads and bridges. Special bridges, called aqueducts, carried water to cities.

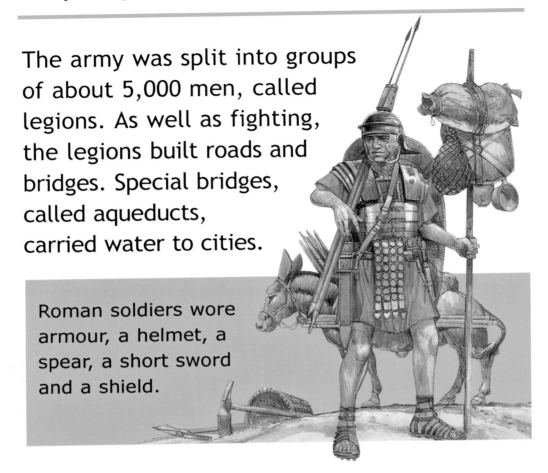

Roman soldiers wore armour, a helmet, a spear, a short sword and a shield.

The Romans also built machines to destroy the walls of enemy cities. One of these threw big stones as far as 300 metres.

When a new land was won, the Romans took stolen gold and silver, slaves, and taxes back to Rome. They also used some of this money to build new towns in the lands they had won.

The Roman Empire

Buildings • Roads • Science • Trade • Latin

The Romans ruled one of the biggest empires ever. Luckily, they were great organisers.

They sent officers everywhere to collect taxes and introduce the Roman way of doing things. No one likes paying taxes — and the Romans taxed everything. The Emperor Vespasian (say "vess-pay-zian") even taxed toilets!

People *did* like the nice things that the Romans brought. The Romans built temples, stadiums, public baths and sewers all over the empire.

The Romans built many roads. These made it easy to move about.

In cold countries, the Romans warmed up their houses by pumping steam under the floors.

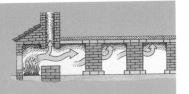

The Romans borrowed their science from the Greeks. They used big machines to lift heavy objects, and the power of water to grind corn.

Roman doctors used herbs for drugs and were very good at healing injuries. Many Romans believed in magical cures and ancient spells.

Wheels were linked with heavy stones that ground corn into flour and squeezed the oil from olives.

Can you see the waterwheel in the picture above? It is still being used to make olive oil.

The Romans even organised time. Each month was divided into three parts and there was a day off work every nine days.

People liked the Romans because they brought peace and made it easy to move goods around.

In Rome, you could buy corn from Egypt, cotton from India, marble from North Africa, silk from China and pearls from Britain.

Ships came from all over the empire to Rome's ports.

In the market place, called the forum, people did their shopping, met for business or just stopped for a chat.

In the centre of every Roman town was a large square. This was the forum. Here you might find people from Rome, Spain, Arabia, Greece, Africa and Gaul (Roman France).

As well as their own language, many people spoke the Roman language, Latin. This made it easier for them to trade with each other.

The modern languages of France, Italy and Spain all come from Latin. Many popular English words also come from Latin — words like "explosion", "joke" and "person".

Towns all over the empire had their own forums, baths and stadiums. Can you guess what this building is? Answer on page 32.

Daily Life

Citizens • Slaves • Families • Houses • Food

Rich Romans made their money from their land and farms. The Romans with good jobs were craft workers, traders and officials. Most people were poor, but if they were citizens they got free food.

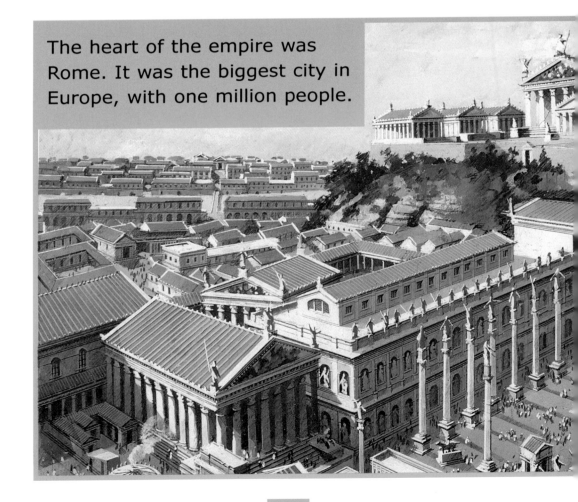

The heart of the empire was Rome. It was the biggest city in Europe, with one million people.

A citizen is a full member of a country. In Rome, only a citizen could vote or own land.

Roman laws protected the citizens. If someone hurt a Roman citizen or stole from them, they were punished. So people all over the empire wanted to become citizens.

Slaves were bought and sold like animals. Most of them were captured in wars.

Slaves had no power at all. They belonged to rich Romans, who often treated them very badly. However, some slaves did become free.

Slaves were often forced to do dangerous jobs, like working in the mines. Others worked in gangs with their feet in chains.

A Roman family was ruled by the father. His wife, children and slaves all had to obey him.

Roman women were not equal with men. They couldn't get good jobs and couldn't vote. Women worked very hard running their homes. They often had lots of children.

Only rich boys went to school. Here they learned how to read and write, and how to speak in public. Other children were taught at home — or not at all.

Most Romans wore simple tunics which hung down to their knees. They also wore boots or sandals (right).

Roman citizens wore large sheets wrapped around their bodies (left). These were called togas.

Roman flats were very crowded.

Rich and poor Romans lived very different lives.

The poor lived in blocks of flats, but there was no heating, water or toilets.

Rich Roman families had large houses in the country, called villas. These were built around open courtyards, with farms attached.

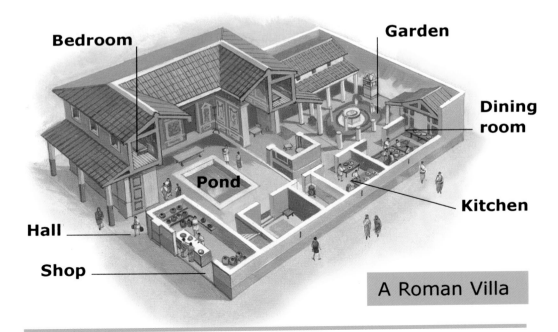

Bedroom

Garden

Dining room

Pond

Kitchen

Hall

Shop

A Roman Villa

20

The streets were dirty, noisy and dangerous. At night, they were very dark. Travellers had to find their way with small lamps.

Poor Romans had to fetch water from wells or fountains in the street, and most of them had no kitchen. Like today, people often ate hot snacks from fast-food shops instead of cooking.

What's the writing on the wall? See answer on page 32.

At the gym, Romans used to keep fit, wash and swim. The gym was also a place to meet friends for a chat.

Everyone stopped for lunch at noon. This was followed by a short rest, called a siesta. People in hot countries such as Spain still do this today.

Oil

Rich people spent their day relaxing at the baths or meeting their friends. At the baths, there was no soap. People used metal scrapers and oil to scrub off the dirt.

Scrapers

Poor Romans worked until sunset, then went to bed after a short meal.

Rich Romans held big feasts. They lay on couches around a low table.

Wild pig

Some ate special dishes like wild pig stuffed with birds.

The Romans ate with their hands and used knives to cut up food. Rich Romans ate a meal with courses of vegetables, meat, fish and cakes. Greedy Romans often made themselves sick, then started eating again!

Most people ate sausages or bacon, fresh vegetables and beans, with fish sauce. The poorest Romans lived on porridge made from bread boiled in water.

Games and Gods

Chariots • Gladiators • Temples • The End

The Roman emperors gave out free food and put on big shows for the people of Rome. They wanted to keep them happy so that they did not become violent and cause trouble.

The Romans liked fighting skills and loved violence. Huge crowds went to see the chariot races. People also watched bloody fights — like we go to watch sports today.

Chariot drivers had to be very skilful to keep their horses under control.

One stadium, the Colosseum, could be filled with water for a sea battle.

Men and women called gladiators fought each other to the death. They also fought against wild animals such as tigers, rhinos and elephants.

At the end of the fight, the crowd booed or cheered the loser. If the emperor pointed his thumb down, the gladiator lived. If he pointed toward his chest, the gladiator died.

Rich Romans liked watching plays and reading poetry. They also loved having paintings, statues and mosaics in their houses.

Big fights happened on festival days. These days were very important to most Romans. They believed that the gods had power over their lives.

In the temples, priests tried to please the gods with gifts and prayers. At home, ordinary Romans prayed to statues of their family gods.

The Romans believed in many gods. The twelve most important were borrowed from the Greeks. Jupiter, the king of the Roman gods, was the same as the Greek god Zeus.

Priests prayed to the gods in the Pantheon, a big temple in Rome.

Foreigners could keep their own gods as long as they also prayed to the emperor. The Christians believed in only one god. Many emperors did not like this and punished them.

Slowly, more and more Romans, especially women, slaves and foreigners, believed in the Christian ideas. In the end, the Christians lived freely.

In later years, the Roman empire faced many problems. Foreign invaders like the Huns attacked the empire and destroyed Rome.

Rome was still the centre of the Christian religion. It was built again about 500 years ago. Rome is now the capital of Italy. If you go there today, you can still see the old forum, once the centre of the world — one world.

Many Christians were burned to death or fed to lions in the Colosseum.

Find Out More

The ideas and inventions of the Romans are still around us. Can you remember what they are? Below are a few pictures which should give you some clues. Turn to page 32 to find out the answers.

UNUSUAL WORDS

Here we explain some words you may have read in this book.

Arch A curved part of a building. Roman builders used arches to hold up roofs or bridges.

Citizen Someone who is a member of a country. Most people today are citizens of the country they are born in.

Emperor The ruler of an empire.

Empire When one strong country rules lots of others.

Forum The main square in a Roman town, used as a market.

Gladiators People who fight for other people to watch. Many gladiators were slaves who were forced to fight each other.

Latin The language of the Ancient Romans.

Legion A group of 5,000 men in the Roman army.

Republic A country with no king. Many modern countries are republics.

Senate The rich men who decided the laws in Ancient Rome.

Toga A white sheet worn by Roman citizens. They wrapped their togas around their bodies.

Villa A large Roman house, usually in the country.

Constantinople

The Emperor Constantine built a new Roman capital and called it Constantinople (left). This city lasted for 1,000 years after Rome was destroyed and kept the Roman ideas alive.

The Planets

The planets in our solar system are named after the Roman gods. Venus was the Roman goddess of love, and Jupiter was the king of the gods.

Venus   **Jupiter**

Roman Numbers

Roman numbers are still used on clocks and for dates. If XVII (X + VII) is 17, what is LXXV? Answer on page 32.

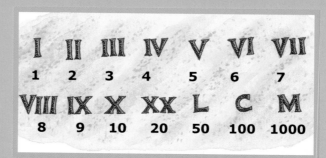

I	II	III	IV	V	VI	VII
1	2	3	4	5	6	7

VIII	IX	X	XX	L	C	M
8	9	10	20	50	100	1000

Who Came First?

Egyptians	Greeks	Romans	Vikings	Present Day

4,000 years ago	2,500 years ago	2,000 years ago	1,000 years ago	Now

Index

ANSWERS TO PICTURE QUESTIONS

Page 15 It's a theatre, from a city in North Africa.
Page 21 Like today, some Romans liked to write their names on the wall (the word for this, "graffiti", comes from Latin). They also wrote rude messages.
Page 30 We use these Roman ideas:

1 Money that can be used in many countries, like the Euro. **2** Many modern buildings look like Roman ones — like the US Senate here. **3** A system of roads. **4** Public swimming pools. **5** The Roman calendar. **6** Names of planets.
Page 31 LXXV is 50 + 20 + 5 = 75.

Illustrators: Stephen Sweet – SGA, Pete Roberts, Steve Caldwell, Norma Burgin – Allied Artists, Peter Kesteven, Dave Burroughs, Gerald Wood, Stephen Sweet, Ivan Lapper, Mike Lacey.
Photocredits: *Abbreviations: l-left, c-centre.* Cover - Digital Stock; 1, 3, 9, 15 & 30l – Spectrum Colour Library; 12 – Charles De Vere; 26 – Eye Ubiquitous; 30c – James Davis Travel Photography.